A Wife is a
Terrible Thing to
Waste

A WIFE IS A TERRIBLE THING TO WASTE

How to love, and live happily and
contented with your contentious wife.

Mr X

Highly Recommended
Barbados

A WIFE IS A TERRIBLE THING TO WASTE
How to love, and live happily and
contented with your contentious wife

CONTENTS

PREFACE – Why I Wrote this Book • vii

INTRODUCTION – What is a Contentious Wife? • ix

Step 1 – No One Is To Blame • 1

Step 2 – Love Your Wife • 3

Step 3 - Understand Your Wife • 7

Step 4 – Listen To Your Wife • 9

Step 5 – Just Do Your Best • 11

Step 6 – Refuse To Argue • 13

Step 7 – Flirt With Your Wife • 15

Step 8 – Restoring A Severed Trust • 17

GRADUATION • 21

ANNEX A • 23

ANNEX B • 25

PREFACE

Why I Wrote This Book

For obvious reasons, I cannot reveal my true identity, otherwise I would soon become Mr Ex - as in ex-husband. For this reason, I cannot attend book tours, radio or television interviews, or any other type of book promotional marketing event where my wife can identify me.

I do not know of any man who would want his wife to know that he was reading this book. Even I would not risk leaving it lying around at home – which is the reason for camouflaging the book's cover. So I have come to accept that this book will bring me neither fame nor fortune. Then why write it?

If you are in an unhappy relationship with your contentious wife, then I wrote this book for you. If you follow the few simple steps in this book, then based on the perfect record of success thus far, I can guarantee that you can love, and be contented and happy with your contentious wife. How can I make such a bold claim?

Like all men married to contentious wives, I became convinced that my wife was the most contentious and angry woman that had ever lived upon the earth.

I love my wife dearly and would do anything for her. However, her constant complaining and arguing about any and everything had literally drained me to the edge of my life. Stumbling around in that nebulous state, I had a moment of clarity and saw a path out of my miserable reality.

I followed the path and soon reached a state of happy contentment with, and unbridled love for my wonderfully contentious wife. She responded by becoming noticeably less contentious.

I taught other men how to enjoy this marital bliss, and all of them have reported that they are still happily married as of the writing of this book. Now it's your turn.

Sincerely,

Mr X

Introduction

What Is A Contentious Woman?

Rather than attempting a complete definition of a contentious woman, let me borrow Solomon's description of what her husband would normally suffer.

> *Better to dwell in a corner of a housetop, than in a house shared with a contentious woman. (Proverbs 21:9)*

> *Better to dwell in the wilderness, than with a contentious and angry woman. (Proverbs 21:19)*

> *A continual dripping on a very rainy day and a contentious woman are alike. (Proverbs 27:15)*

If this describes your life, then this book is for you. If not, then be very grateful for your good fortune and please keep your advice to yourself. Because you simply cannot understand what we are going through, and your well-intentioned advice on what we should and should not do to improve our marriages is, frankly, annoying – I tried them and they did not work.

I remember reading those Proverbs about a contentious woman when I was 14 years old, and determined then that I would avoid a contentious bride at all costs. When I was dating my bride to be, I consciously assessed the risk that she would be contentious after we were married, and I concluded, with a high level of confidence, that the risk was exceedingly low. With that hurdle out of the way, we got married.

Soon after our honeymoon, I began to observe unmistakable signs of contentious behaviours, and their frequency increased with time. For the first 6 months, she was contentious approximately once each month, then twice each month, then weekly, then twice each week, then daily, and finally multiple times each day. Often, she would be contentious from the time that she opened her eyes in the morning until she closed them at night. Sometimes, she would awake in the middle of the night, wake me to quarrel about something or the other, and then go back to sleep.

Initially, I was amused at her outbursts. Then alarmed and concerned about the increasingly frequent complaints, criticisms and loud arguments. When their frequency reached daily, it began to drain my energy and motivation. I found that I could no longer do household chores and had to hire others to do what I used to do. My every suggestion or idea would be ridiculed and I would be discouraged to the point of not even trying.

I began breaking emotionally under the load of contentious criticism and arguments, and I lost a considerable amount of weight. I visited my doctor who declared that my measurements were off of his Body-Mass Index chart. He did tests for a diverse range of diseases, all of which came back negative. I began to feel that I was hovering near the edge of my life, and began to put my house in order. Then, in a moment of clarity I saw a path out of my depressed state.

I followed the path to happiness and contentment with my angry and contentious wife, and can finally tick "happily married" on those marriage surveys. Admittedly, I struggled with accepting and implementing each step but my stubbornness only delayed my happiness.

If you are contemplating divorce, or have resigned to a lifetime sentence of marital unhappiness, then congratulations, you hold the keys to your deliverance in your hands. Let me show you the way out of your apathetic disillusionment.

Before we start, you must satisfy the following two prerequisites:

1) you must want a happy and contented relationship with your contentious wife; and

2) you must be honest with yourself.

So let me ask you, do you honestly want to be happy and contented with your contentious wife? If your answer is "Yes", then go to Step 1 without delay – you should love, and be happily contented with your wife in about 30 days if you follow the steps[1]. If not, then put this book down until the three Proverbs quoted at the beginning of this Introduction describe your marriage relationship.

---

[1] Some men who had engaged in harmful addictive behavior have reported a longer period.

STEP 1

No One Is To Blame

The first step to marital happiness is to stop blaming someone else for the miserable state that you are in. Do not blame your parents, siblings, in-laws, friends, wife, God or yourself. There is nothing that you could have done to avoid choosing a contentious wife. Marriage is like a lottery, and you do not know the type of wife whom you will draw. It is not your or anyone else's fault that you happened to select a contentious bride. All I can say is - welcome to the club. Now let us see how you got here.

Before I got married, I thought that I knew my fiancée well, and she thought that she knew me well also. But we did not know each other because we were too busy trying to present a good impression. If we revealed our repulsive bad habits during the time that we were enjoying being attracted to each other, then we probably would never have gotten married.

I do not think that any couple can know how similar or different their spouses will be to the person whom they courted regardless of their marriage preparations. We knew each other for over a decade, attended pre-marriage counselling, and engaged in role playing situational exercises and games to remove any 'masks' that may have prevented us from knowing who we were going to marry. I also spoke to all of her siblings and some of her close friends. Yet, I still selected the most contentious wife available despite consciously and actively trying not to do so.

After my wife' arguments and complaints became daily and unbearable, I secretly blamed: her for tricking me, her parents for raising a contentious daughter, and God for not stopping the marriage; but my blaming improved nothing.

The first step on the road to happy contentment is to purposefully accept that no one is to blame for your selection of a contentious wife. Say to yourself, especially when your wife is being contentious, or when you feel the temptation to blame others:

"I blame no-one for selecting a contentious wife."

You may accept this immediately or after a few days, but once you do, then you will have a strong foundation on which to support the other steps. See you over in Step 2.

STEP 2

Love Your Wife

I was convinced, beyond any shadow of doubt, that I loved my bride. I felt carefree, happy, and excited, and our honeymoon was perfect – far beyond what I had imagined. One year later, after she could restrain her contentious ways no longer, I thought that I must have loved her, because I was obviously blind to this behaviour before we got married.

Admittedly, I did some things to initiate our arguments. But I considered such arguments to be a normal part of any marriage. I did not expect continual contention.

In my near death moment of clarity, I realized that it was possible that I never actually loved my wife. I rejected this thought for months and only succeeded in needlessly extending my suffering, since nothing had changed except not blaming anyone for my misery. You are probably convinced that you also loved your wife before you were married. So allow me to explain my new understanding of love, and then you can decide for yourself.

Attraction

I have been attracted to how a woman wears her clothes and her hair, and how she walks, smells, talks and reads. I have also been attracted to her skill at a sport, or playing a musical instrument, or singing. I can be attracted to the sound of her laughter, or the attention that she commands when organising a team. There are perhaps an infinite number of things that can attract me to a woman.

I have found that while I am in this state of attraction, I can minimize the importance of things about her that I would normally find repulsive. I may be attracted to her skill at playing volleyball, but not to her tendency to shout obscenities. While I noticed such repulsive behaviour, I tended to minimize its importance, or excuse it as her being intense, or convincing myself that it is a habit that she will learn to discard.

I have been attracted to many women. However, I am not now attracted to most of them. My attraction to them was initially quite intense – so much so that I would day and night dream about them. However, over time, the intensity of my attraction subsided.

Most of the women to whom I was attracted never knew me. Some of them never said more than a polite greeting. However, there were a few with whom I conversed – and developed a bond.

Bonding

Our bond grew strong as we shared stories about events in our lives – emotional stories. Our bond also grew strong as we visited places together. We developed a close friendship. However, over time, the intensity of my attraction for her would subside, and some of her attributes that I found least attractive would begin, somehow, to take on greater importance. Her behaviour that I had previously justified as being cute and unique became irritating. My changing reaction always confused and disturbed me.

Love

I found that attraction was easy and required no effort on my part – I just enjoyed the pleasurable feelings that watching or thinking about her generated within me. Bonding required some effort - and money. Love was difficult and required much effort.

Many of my friends were contented to enjoy the excitements of attraction, or the benefits of bonding. However, they seemed unprepared to make the investment that love demanded.

When the intense feelings of attraction waned, and I was confronted with the good, bad and ugly about her, it was then that I was faced with the choice to love her.

I define love as the decision to accept a person exactly as she is, with all of her repulsive habits, while at the same time creating an environment where she can thrive.

Do you love your wife? Do you accept her exactly as she is, 'warts and all'? I know that this is not easy, especially if you are married to a woman who has 'let herself go'. If you are like me, then you may feel tempted to blame her again – for not taking care of herself. However, if you have reached this step, we have already agreed to stop blaming.

Are you ready to accept her exactly as she is – contentious behaviour and all? Are you willing to accept her whether she changes for the better or worse?

Once you have decided to accept her just as she is, then we can move on to the next steps where you can create an environment where she can grow and thrive.

Step 3

Understand Your Wife

Dwell with them with understanding. (1 Peter 3:7)

Ok, let's try a little exercise. Circle one person whom you honestly believe is responsible for you marrying a contentious wife: a parent, sibling, in-law, friend, wife, God, satan, or yourself. If you circled any choice, then you need to return to Step 1, otherwise, let us continue.

A man can marry one of the following types of women:

- contented and grateful;

- discontented and grateful;

- discontented and ungrateful.

Normally within two years of marriage, a man should be able to identify the type of wife he has chosen. The man who has selected a wife who is both contented with, and grateful for what she has, is very fortunate indeed. I used to envy such men, and be intensely angry with them whenever they seemed to take these angels for granted.

The man who loves and marries a woman who is grateful with what she has, but who always wants more, will try in vain to make her contented. However, her gratefulness with what she already has will encourage the man and give him an illusionary hope that one day her insatiable needs will be satisfied. A man who marries such a woman may go into an unsustainable debt, and work himself to death trying to please her.

The man who is unlucky enough to have drawn a discontented and ungrateful wife has significant challenges. If he loves her, he may labour in vain to try to please her. However, since she gives him no encouragement, he may eventually stop trying. Such a wife will quickly lose respect for her husband and even teach their children to also.

Please do not be discouraged if this mirror provides some clarity to your situation. Since you are actually reading this book, you are already on the path to a fulfilling marriage. Once you have identified whether you have a grateful or ungrateful discontented wife, then it is time to use this information in Step 4.

Step 4

Listen To Your Wife

A contentious wife is likely to be discontented with everything that she has and every service that she receives. There is nothing that you can do to make her content – only God can change her. Even if you had one billion US dollars in your bank account to spend on her, your wife will not be contented. She will tend to exhibit contentious and angry behaviour no matter what you do, or do not do.

It should liberate you to know that you cannot satisfy your contentious wife with material possessions, or the quality of your services – but you should try.

This Step consists of bearing with her complaints long enough to write the items that she is complaining about every day. If your wife is not complaining every day yet, then you can wait until she does, or you can write the items that she is complaining about every week. If she is not complaining every week, then perhaps you do not have a contentious wife.

Once you have this list, then place the items in three categories, namely: Habitual, Affordable, and Unaffordable as shown in the following table, and provided for your use in Annex B.

Habitual	Affordable	Unaffordable

In the Habitual category, list your behaviours that she frequently complains about. These may be habits like leaving the toilet seat up, or placing dishes in the 'wrong' location, or not putting away your clothes, etc, etc. These are things that you can easily do without spending any money.

In the Affordable category, list the items which you can afford to complete with your available resources. In the Unaffordable category, list the items that you cannot complete unless you go into debt.

You should repeat this step at least annually, or as your cash flow projections may suggest, for as long as you both shall live. Now, on to Step 5.

Step 5

Just Do Your Best

Your responsibility is not to pursue an impossible and illusionary goal of satisfying her every want, but a realistic and achievable one of doing your best and no more. More than your best means that you are using someone else's resources, thereby getting into debt.

You are responsible for doing the items listed in the Habitual and Affordable categories. You can ignore the items in the Unaffordable category for now. When you repeat Step 4 next year, or earlier, then you may have obtained enough resources to move some items from the Unaffordable category to the Affordable.

This Step consists of prioritizing the items in the Habitual and Affordable categories, and agreeing to do at least one task from each of them each week. Once the task is done, then you should cross it off of your list. Your grateful contentious wife will likely thank you. Your ungrateful contentious may belittle your efforts, which is her default response and is to be expected. However, if your ungrateful contentious wife attempts to show some gratitude, even if the attempt is poorly made, then encourage her. Tell her: *"Your gratitude means a lot to me."*

When your wife complains that you have not done something in the Unaffordable category, then you should gently explain to her that the unaffordable task will be done when you have saved enough money to afford to complete it. You will thus avoid the stress that accompanies being in debt.

When you became a husband and father, you automatically became responsible for protecting, sheltering, clothing and feeding your family. If you are unable to fulfil these basic responsibilities on your own, then ask for help from your extended family, friends, and God.

Your basic responsibilities are as if you and your wife were in a canoe [a small boat], and both of you had paddles. If you have a contentious wife, then she may refuse to paddle, and spend her time criticising your best efforts. But you must resolve to do your best. You must keep paddling regardless of what she does, says, or does not do. However, if you follow the Steps in this book, then you can paddle while being happily contented with your contentious wife. Now, on to Step 6.

STEP 6

Refuse To Argue

A contentious and angry wife will tend to argue and complain loudly. After our honeymoon, my wife used to 'blow up' once each month. It gradually increased to multiple times each day.

Initially, some action of mine would provoke a shouting match. However, when the frequency of her arguments became daily, she would simply start a loud argument without any provocation or input from me.

I began to be concerned about the impact that her frequent outbursts and belittling were having on our growing children. I was also concerned about the impact that her constant complaints were having on my health. I should note that after I implemented this step, the frequency of my wife's outbursts reduced significantly. This is what I did.

Whenever my wife would start shouting, I would calmly but firmly tell her that I refuse to participate in a shouting match with her, and I refuse to argue with her in front of our children – then I would calmly walk away. Seeing their father assert himself this way let my children know that *'Daddy is in the house'*.

Initially, my wife just continued shouting at me as I walked away. But after one week of watching me calmly walking away, she stopped shouting as much. We went from having an explosive ding-dong multiple times each day to one every two weeks - sweet. I have come to accept that her nature compels her to 'blow off some steam' at least once or twice each month.

I know that it is difficult to hear your wife's constant criticisms and belittling for too long without responding or even storming off, but try these simple exercises.

1. Breathe deeply and slowly, and do not respond while as she is shouting. It is easy to say regrettable things in anger.

2. Concentrate on your heart beat, and be encouraged by these words from God: *'In quietness and confidence shall be your strength.' (Isaiah 30:15)*

This action of not participating in a shouting match does not preclude having a discussion when she is calmer; but when the shouting starts, just walk away. This may take a few weeks, but be persistent and patient.

STEP 7

Flirt With Your Wife

Let her breasts satisfy you at all times; and always be enraptured with her love. (Proverbs 5:19)

Well, you have been through a lot and now it is time for your reward. Let us see how far you have come over the past month.

- You have stopped blaming anyone for choosing a contentious wife and you have accepted that there is nothing that you or anyone could have done to prevent it – it is what it is.

- You have accepted your wife exactly as she is.

- You have accepted that there is nothing that you can do to make your wife content with material possessions or services, and you have resolved to simply do your best, and not get into debt.

- You have listened to her complaints, agreed to do only what you can afford, and have determined to complete one habitual and affordable task each week.

- You have refused to participate in shouting matches with your wife, and have learnt to avoid the stresses associated with her frequent complaints.

Well done. By unconditionally accepting her as she is, and creating an environment where she can thrive by completing things on your Habitual and Affordable lists, you have demonstrated your love for her. Now - your reward.

Every day, even on the days when she explodes, you must flirt with your wife at least 3 times each day: morning, before dinner, and before you go to bed. Whenever she is at the kitchen counter, hug her from behind and gently caress her belly and breasts while you kiss her shoulder and neck. At night, gently massage her feet with massage oil.

Caress her breasts and buttocks under her clothes whenever she is inviting you by walking around without her bra or panties.

Whenever she is lying down, caress and kiss her inner thighs and breasts, and let her invite you in. Be patient and persistent, but whatever happens, keep working on your lists.

STEP 8

Restoring a Severed Trust

At this time, we need to address the 800 pound gorilla in the room – what about if your marital trust was severed by marital infidelity, or misuse of joint funds, or some other major issue?

Once trust has been severed, it can only be restored if the offended party forgives the repentant party – there is no other way.

If you are not the offended party, then you must position yourself to be forgiven. Therefore, you must be repentant and demonstrate that you are repentant. If you are the offended party, and if she is repentant, then you must forgive her if you want the bond of trust restored.

Forgiveness means that the offended gives up their right to hold the offence against the offender. This is very difficult to do on your own, but many have found that cultivating a relationship with God had facilitated the process.

Cultivating a relationship with God is a lot easier than it sounds. You can initiate the process right now. If you are serious, then simply say: *"God, I want to know you and follow you. Please show me how."* and He will - guaranteed.

Restoring a Damaged Trust

The 800 pound gorilla's little brother is pornography, alcoholism, drugs, or any other harmful addictive behaviour. These behaviours damage the trust, and if not stopped, will eventually sever it.

Once you have been addicted to a harmful behaviour, you will likely remain vulnerable to repeating it for the remainder of your life. Fortunately, there is a solution.

First, believe that your addictive behaviour is very harmful to your marriage and family. It will sever the trust with your wife, and almost guarantee that your children will have to struggle with the same addictions.

Second, once you have accepted that your behaviour is harmful, then determine to stop it for your sake and your family's.

Third, demonstrate both your belief and determination with action. You are currently in a fight with your body, and your body has the advantage of a consistent record of winning. You need time to heal the damaged trust between you and the rest of your family, and to strengthen your resolve to win. You can gain the advantage by avoiding all potential confrontations with your body.

Five, to avoid the foreseeable confrontations, you must destroy all materials in your home that has caused you to fail. This may mean destroying books and magazines, flushing substances down the toilet, and deleting computer images. You must demonstrate that you are a champion in your house.

Six, if you watch pornography on your computer, whether at work or home, then you can gain the advantage by fighting in the light. Explain to your wife that the risk of unintentionally looking at pornography on the Internet, or when opening electronic mail, is high. Explain that the sight of her naked body is the only sexually explicit image that you want to see, and the only one stored in your mind. Then install a computer filter on all computers that you use and let her be the only person to enter and know the password.

Seven, if you watch pornography when you are alone in a hotel room, then either always travel with your wife, or ensure that the television is removed from your room. Ask the hotel and they will do it. If the addictive behaviour is alcohol or drugs, then never travel without your wife, or a responsible male relative who can share your room. You must do this because you know, based on prior battles, that you will likely fail if you are alone.

If you fall along the way, then acknowledge that you have failed, turn back towards the light and keep trying. You should know that you have already won, because you are no longer embracing what you know to be harmful. Rather, you have chosen to embrace what is good and helpful, and resist what is harmful.

You may have to continue resisting previously addictive desires until the day that you die, so do not stop fighting. The frequency of your battles depends on your decision to remain in an advantageous position by keeping the addictive materials out of your home – your place of safety. If you allow them in, then you will have more unnecessary battles to fight, and potentially to lose.

If you win at home, you will likely win when you are confronted with the temptations outside of your home.

GRADUATION

I guaranteed that you would be happily contented with your contentious wife if you followed the steps provided in this book. Many have found this happiness and there is no reason why you should not as well. The only reason why you may not be happy at this point is if you are still complaining. Let me explain.

To be happily contented requires one critical ingredient - thankfulness. You cannot be happy and ungrateful at the same time. You also cannot be thankful and complain at the same time. Your happiness depends on your decision to be thankful, and the expression of that decision by not complaining.

Please, resolve not to complain about your wife to anyone, because your complaining will effectively block your feelings of happiness. If your wife is aware of your complaints, then that that will be as repulsive to her as her complaining is to you.

You must also thank someone for your wife, and the best person to thank is the one who joined you together. Remember these words of Jesus that are normally spoken at weddings?

> *Therefore what God has joined together, let not man separate." (Matthew 19:6)*

Therefore, tell God how grateful you are for your wife. With God on your side, you can only benefit.

If you have read every page in this book, then please answer the questions in Annex A to check whether you have completed every step successfully. If you have, then congratulations.

Thank you for reading, and I hope that it has significantly improved your relationship with your wife.

If you have followed all of the steps, and you would like to encourage others with your story, or if you have some questions or would like further information about anything presented in this book, then you are welcome to visit me at:

HappilyContented.wordpress.com.

Sincerely,

Mr X.

Annex A

Please answer the following questions honestly. Use your responses to improve your marriage where necessary.

1. Who do you blame for being married to a contentious wife?

2. Have you accepted your wife, exactly as she is, with all of her faults and her contentious nature?

3. Does your wife express gratitude or ingratitude for the responsible things that you do for her?

4. Have you written the list of things that your wife complains about in Annex B? If you cannot fill both pages, then your wife may not be very contentious.

5. Are you doing your best and no more?

6. Have you completed at least one page of the habitual and Affordable items in Annex B?

7. Have you decided to delay the Unaffordable things that your wife wants (not needs) until you can afford to do them without getting into debt?

8. Have you consistently stopped engaging in a shouting match with your wife, and calmly walked away when she started?

9. Have you consistently stopped arguing with your wife in front of your children?

10. Have you spent one month completing items in Annex B before flirting with your wife? Please note that you should always release her if she pulls away, but always return to hug her later that day. Do not see it as rejection, but a component of a life-long love dance.

11. Have you forgiven her for everything she has done and said to you, especially during loud arguments?

12. Have you put yourself in a position to be forgiven by her? If so, then have you asked her for forgiveness?

13. Are you complaining about your wife to any one?

14. Are you resisting addictive behaviours as recommended?

15. Have you told God how thankful you are to be married to your wife?

16. Are you cultivating a relationship with your Creator?

Annex B

Complete the following list categories.

Habitual	Affordable	Unaffordable

Habitual	Affordable	Unaffordable

Use additional paper as necessary.